PHANTOMS IN THE ARK

FANTASMAS EN EL ARCA

PHANTOMS IN THE ARK

FANTASMAS EN EL ARCA

. . . imagen era él, yacente, para sí mismo y, rumbo hacia la realidad más real, llevado por ondas invisibles, sumergiéndose en ellas, era la imagen de la nave su propia imagen; de la oscuridad viniendo, a la oscuridad llevando, hundiéndose en la oscuridad, él mismo era la inconmensurable nave, el único inconmensurable, y él era también la huída dirigida hacia este inconmensurable, él mismo la nave fugitiva, él mismo la meta, inconmensurable él mismo, inconmensurable, inborrablemente presente, infinito paisaje corporal el paisaje de su cuerpo, imagen poderosa y amplia del inframundo de la noche . . .

—Hermann Broch
La muerte de Virgilio

. . . yo soy mi propio enemigo-fantasma—y este Monstruo debe morir . . .

—Peter Handke
El peso del mundo

. . . an image to himself was he who lay there, and steering toward the most real reality, borne on invisible waves, dipping into them, the image of the ship was his own image emerging from darkness, heading towards darkness, sinking into darkness, he himself was the boundless ship that at the same time was boundlessness; and he himself was the flight that was aiming towards this boundlessness; he was the fleeing ship, he himself the goal, he himself was boundlessness too vast to be seen, unimaginable, an endless corporeal landscape, the landscape of his body, a mighty, outspread, infernal image of night . . .

—Hermann Broch
The Death of Virgil

. . . I myself am my phantom-enemy—and this Monster must die . . .

—Peter Handke
The Weight of the World

They woke with pieces of memories: fighting,
drunkenness, an alley, a burning open door,
asphalt and bloody vomit, youth's kingdom,
many friends, vast thought, spring wind, the freedom
of the streets. But the city rocked, and salt spittle
from the night sky battered it, it plunged and twisted
bound on its way in black water. The streets now,
become corridors and decks, had nowhere to go,
each swallowed its own tail and merged itself
in the others, and the ocean
was at the end of all. A grey slime
thrashed weakly, groping for their ankles,
as they stumbled, seeking out
a lighted place, music, thronged voices hoarse
with pleasure repeating the lives that they recall:

Despertaron con trozos de recuerdos: riñas,
ebriedad, un callejón, una puerta abierta en llamas,
asfalto y vómito sanguinolento, reino de la juventud,
muchos amigos, pensamiento vasto, viento de primavera, la libertad
de la calle. Pero la ciudad se mecía, y la golpeaba
el salivazo salado del cielo nocturno, se precipitaba y retorcía
entremezclado en su correr en el agua negra. Las calles
ahora convertidas en pasillos y cubiertas no hallaban salida,
se tragaban su cola y se fusionaban
una en otra, el océano
al fondo de todo. Un fango gris
se meneaba débilmente, tratando de alcanzar sus tobillos,
mientras tropezaban, buscando
un lugar con luz, música, voces amontonadas roncas
de placer repitiendo las vidas que ellos volvían a llamar:

We met the robot fish-man Sisyphus . . .

We met the robot fish-man Sisyphus
in a bar and laid our hands on him. And so
by law he had to tell us everything
our hearts desired, and thus began:

Encontramos al robot, hombre-pescado Sísifo
en un bar, impusimos nuestras manos sobre él, esa fue
la ley que lo obligó a decirnos todo
hasta hartarnos, y así nos relató:

That day,
as the vehicle approached the crest of the hill . . .

That day,
as the vehicle approached the crest of the hill,
it seemed the slightest touch would incline it toward joy
and we would slide down into the blue valley.

Ese día,
cuando el vehículo se acercaba a lo alto de la colina,
el más leve toque habría podido inclinarlo hacia la alegría
haciéndonos deslizar cuesta abajo al valle azul.

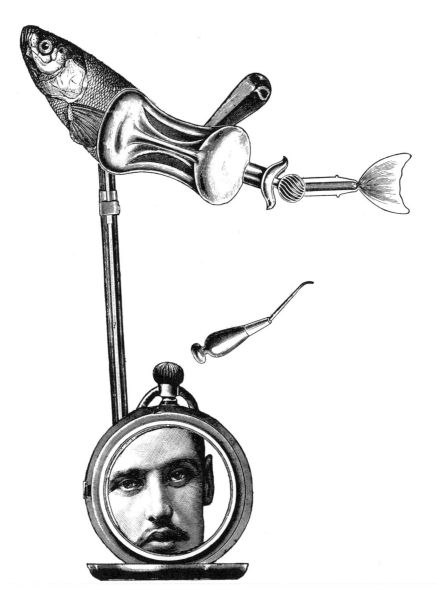

There, all would have been different from this floating life . . .

There, all would have been different from this floating life.
There we saw soil for the hooves, waves for the fins, sky for the wings:
a place to be in. But our motion failed
and we dropped back, gathering speed until

Allá todo habría sido distinto de esta vida flotante.
Ahí vimos tierra para las pezuñas, olas para las aletas, cielo para
las alas:
un lugar para quedarse. Pero nuestro movimiento falló
y caímos hacia atrás, acelerando hasta que

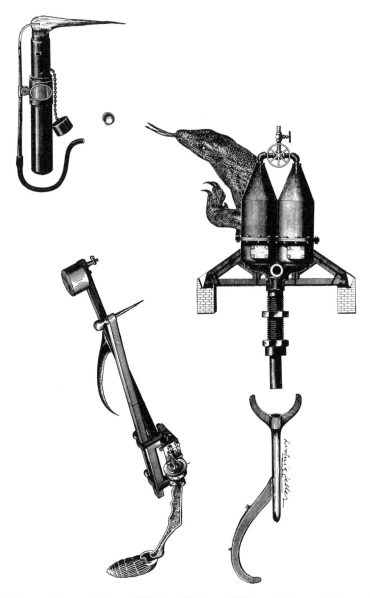

. . . we struck the point of origin
and shattered . . .

we struck the point of origin
and shattered. The pieces flew
in every direction, screws screwing vast spaces,
a thousand springs uncoiling in that fall,
until our parts littered a virgin void,
a vacant lot between auto body shops.

nos estrellamos con el punto de partida
despedazándonos. Los trozos volaron
en todas las direcciones, tornillos retorciendo vastos espacios,
mil resortes desenrollándose en la caída,
hasta que nuestros pedazos se esparcieron en el vacío virgen,
un terreno baldío entre talleres de carrocerías de autos.

There true consciousness was born . . .

There true consciousness was born
in the piles of disconnected gauges reading zero.
The veil was torn and I recalled my infancy at last.
No, there was never a beginning,
never any creation, explosion, first grain or archetype:

Allí nació la verdadera conciencia
entre pilas de manómetros desconectados que indicaban cero.
El velo se rasgó y al fin recordé mi infancia.
No, nunca hubo un comienzo,
nunca hubo una creación, explosión, primer grano o arquetipo:

. . . always, only, these parts . . .

always, only, these parts, no two from the same machine.
They lay all around, then came together a while
and claimed to distinguish joy from suicide.

What was that place—a battlefield or bed—
where yesterday's cut-off limbs kissed one another?
Where was the glory in that squalor,
the destiny in that nervous pile?
I remember words: "When you have lifted me up . . ."
But must the unconscious dust lie and drift
in utter idiocy a billion years
waiting for a hand to gather it?

sólo, siempre, estos trozos, nunca dos de la misma máquina.
Yacían por todas partes, se reunían por un tiempo
y decían poder distinguir la alegría del suicidio.

¿Qué lugar era ese—campo de batalla o lecho—
donde las extremidades cortadas de antaño se besaban?
¿Dónde estaba la gloria en esa miseria,
dónde el destino en ese montón nervioso?
Recuerdo las palabras: "Cuando me alzaste . . ."
Pero ¿debe acaso el polvo inconsciente yacer y correr a la deriva
en estado de total idiotez esperando un billón de años
que una mano lo levante?

Better if here I had been a camel or a goat...

Better if here I had been a camel or a goat
or the slow uncoiling of a watery form.
And so I invented the dream.
For fourteen days and nights I stood upright
in the thornbushes without waking, for fourteen years
I never lay down but always slept
while wandering. For the journey is undertaken
in sleep and joy, but to wake up is to shipwreck
and drown again in the same dusty form
that floods from every dawn. No limit

Mejor me habría sido ser aquí un camello o una cabra
o el lento desenrollarse de una forma acuosa.
De modo que inventé el sueño.
Durante catorce días con sus noches estuve de pie
en las zarzas sin despertar, durante catorce años
nunca me acosté pero siempre dormía
mientras vagaba. Porque el viaje se emprende
en el sueño y en la alegría, pero despertar es naufragar
y ahogarse de nuevo en la misma forma polvorienta
que nos inunda cada amanecer. No hay límite

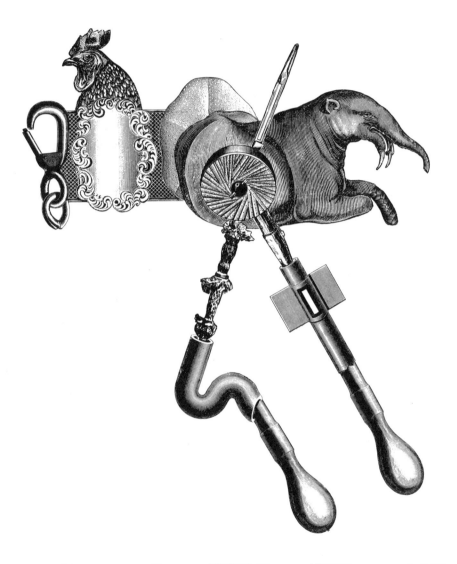

No limit
is set to what human beings may become . . .

is set to what human beings may become.
And I, who come from nowhere, now
I am the tumor of my father. I know
there is no inner life, no seeing of God,
only combination and growth without cause.

para las formas del acontecer de lo humano.
Y yo, que vengo de ninguna parte, soy ahora
el tumor de mi padre. Sé
que no hay vida interior, no se puede ver a Dios,
sólo existe el recombinarse y el crecer sin causa.

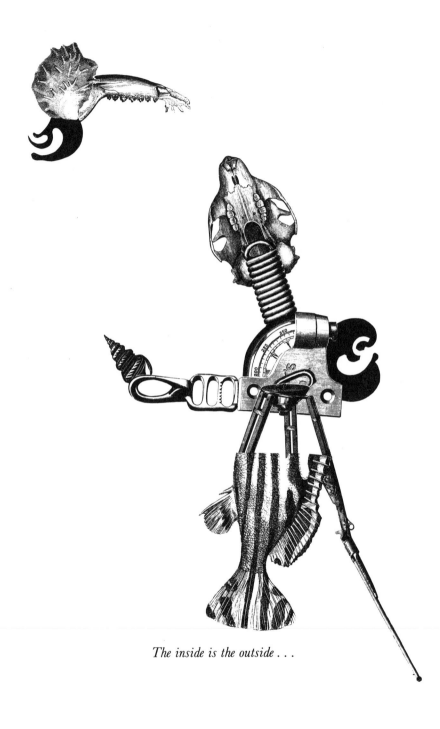

The inside is the outside . . .

The inside is the outside,
watches and springs move between them,
they appear but never are repentant and transformed
within one another. They are always over there.
And so it is better to abandon
the dry Artesian well, my sleep, and better

El interior es el exterior,
relojes y resortes transitan entre ellos,
se hacen evidentes pero nunca se arrepienten ni se transforman
el uno dentro del otro. Están siempre allí.
Y por eso es mejor abandonar
el pozo artesiano seco, mi reposo, y es mejor

. . . to admit I draw the Nile and all its monsters
out of myself . . .

to admit I draw the Nile and all its monsters
out of myself: the Nile that rises in the south
and the heavenly Nile with its god
who sprinkles blue water even down upon
the far-off abominable Kheta. When the weather's bad,
when mist drools on the towers
and the windows dissolve, it's not the earth
that oppresses me: all falls from my self-hatred.
I wish I knew how to quit hating myself
but such days come upon me. Great bolts of anger

admitir que yo hago manar el Nilo y todos sus monstruos
de mí mismo: el Nilo que surge en el Sur
y el Nilo celestial con su dios
que salpica agua azul incluso allá abajo
sobre la lejana abominable Kheta. Cuando hay mal tiempo,
cuando la niebla corre como baba por las torres
y se disuelven las ventanas, no es la tierra
que me oprime: todo proviene del odio a mí mismo.
Quisiera saber cómo dejar de odiarme
pero me sobrevienen días así. Grandes estallidos de ira

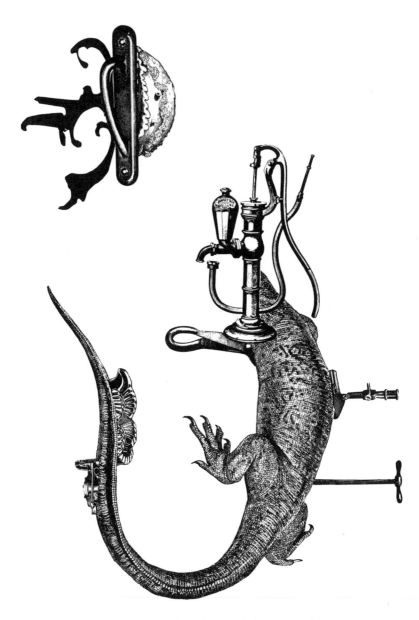

. . .fell the hairs of my head and drive me indoors . . .

fell the hairs of my head and drive me indoors
because I can't imagine a world or a body
in which I could endure to live without end,

as I desire. Is it time? Will I decide at last
to sink my always thirsty shaft into the waves
of granulated stone, to force the water up
and turn it on the lathe, pierce it with rodent drills,
rivet the water, slice it into wheels
and teeth, stars, claws, haunches, gullets, brains?

hacen caer mis cabellos y me arrastran puertas adentro
porque no puedo imaginar un mundo o un cuerpo
en el que soportaría vivir sin fin,

según deseo. ¿Es hora ya? ¿Decidiré al fin
hundir mi dardo siempre sediento en las olas
de piedra granulada, para hacer surgir el agua
y hacerla girar en el torno, horadarla con roedores taladros,
remachar el agua, rebanarla en ruedas
y dientes, estrellas, garras, ancas, gargantas, cerebros?

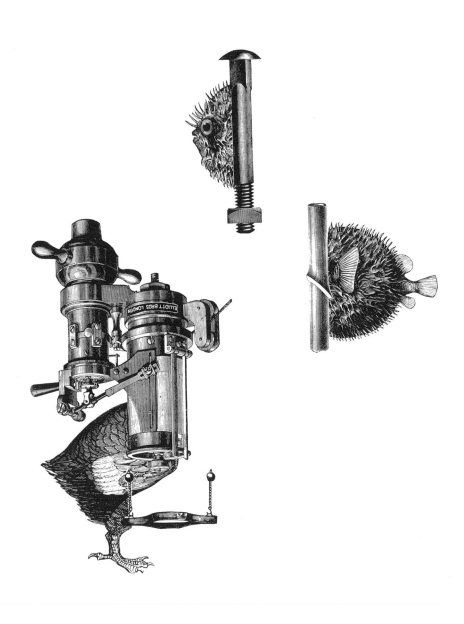

All those old ideas I had in my sleep . . .

All those old ideas I had in my sleep,
hooves, fins and wings, stampeding, swimming, flying:
I could unmake them and begin anew.
For now they torture me, they storm upon me,
flocks and herds and schools in the form of dust on the wind
erode the pink stones.

Todas estas viejas ideas tuve en sueños,
pezuñas, aletas y alas en estampida, a nado, volando:
podía deshacerlas y recomenzar.
Pero ahora son ellas las que me torturan, me asaltan,
bandadas y manadas, cardúmenes cual polvo arrastrado por el viento
erosionan las piedras rosadas.

How can these shadows afflict a shadow so?

How can these shadows afflict a shadow so?
They turn my screws as if they were
the desert earth adjusting the emptiness of its creature,
the tension of an eternally stiff horn.

¿Cómo pueden estas sombras afligir de tal manera una sombra?
Hacen girar mis tornillos como si fueran
la tierra desierta ajustando el vacío de su propia obra,
la tensión de un cuerno eternamente rígido.

I did not always drink so much . . .

I did not always drink so much.
At first I was an exiled poet, busy
and contented in my work. I made again
the past and future according to my desire
as far as the circuitry permitted
and as modified by the acid storms that rise
from Adriatic foam and shells.
I sang how the elements of earth
massed in the all-powerful void
to plant old gardens, and of the god who created wine,
and of those naked storms walking over the land
with bright white feet, crushing the towers,
burning and crumbling the fields.

Yo no siempre tomaba tanto.
Al principio fui un poeta exilado, atareado
y contento de mi trabajo. Rehice
el pasado y el futuro de acuerdo a mi deseo
hasta donde lo permitía el circuito
y según los fueran modificando las tormentas de ácido
alzándose de la espuma y las conchas del Adriático.
Cantaba de cómo los elementos de la tierra
se concentraban en el vacío todopoderoso
para plantar viejos jardines, y canté del dios que creó el vino,
y de esas tormentas desnudas desplazándose sobre el polvo
con blancos pies brillantes, triturando las torres,
quemando y desmenuzando los campos.

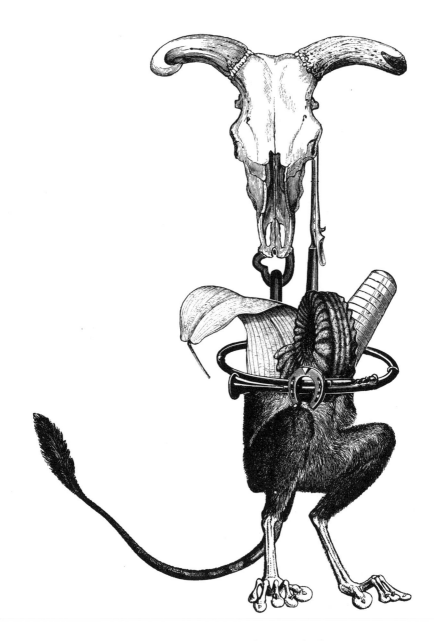

but without plain prose to guide me in the desert . . .

                              I sang,
but without plain prose to guide me in the desert
I soon lost my way and died of thirst
among circles, crosses and pyramids.
When nothing I did came to any end,
I forced it into a few feet in the vastness
until the pressure made it glow. Then I awoke
midway in the journey of our life
on a white table,

                              Yo cantaba,
pero sin prosa llana que me guiase en el desierto
pronto me perdí y perecí de sed
entre círculos, cruces y pirámides.
Cuando el fruto de mi labor acabó en nada
lo empujé a la fuerza a un par de pies en la vastedad
hasta que la presión lo hizo brillar. Entonces desperté
en medio del camino de nuestra vida
en una mesa blanca,

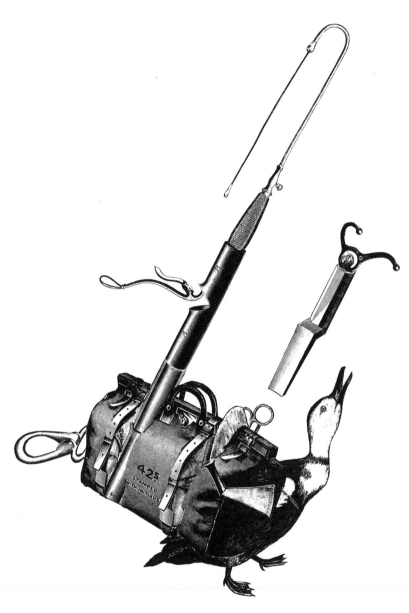

. . . screaming the scalpel . . .

          screaming the scalpel
is just what I always had imagined,
the arclight burning out my eyes,
the surgeon installing a mirror and a lens.

          gritando que el bisturí
es tal como siempre había imaginado,
la luz de arco quemando mis ojos,
el cirujano que instala un espejo y un lente.

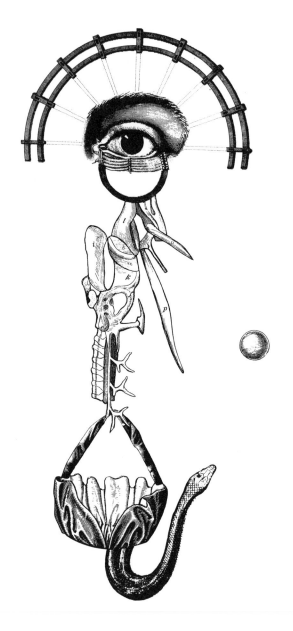

Now what is left of me?

Now what is left of me? I know
nothing about it except that it is God.

¿Ahora qué queda de mí? De ello
nada sé excepto que es Dios.

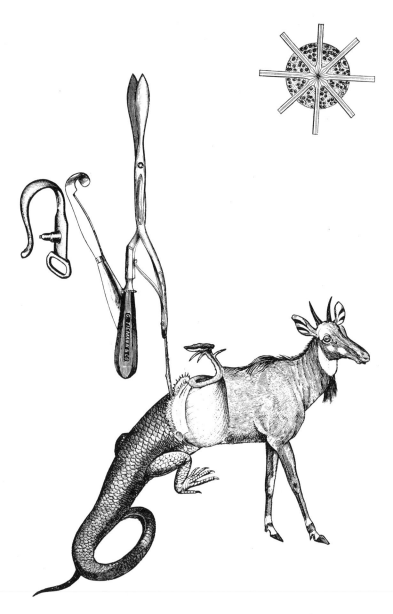

And thus it was that I reluctantly agreed . . .

And thus it was that I reluctantly agreed
to take over my father's failing business:
the bringing forth from nothing
of creatures unheralded, utterly new
beneath a new star, my brain swimming
in a blind, white, absent sea.

Y así, de mala gana acepté
ocuparme del negocio en quiebra de mi padre:
el crear, hacer nacer de la nada
creaturas nunca proclamadas, del todo nuevas
bajo una nueva estrella, con mi cerebro nadando
en un mar ciego, blanco, ausente.

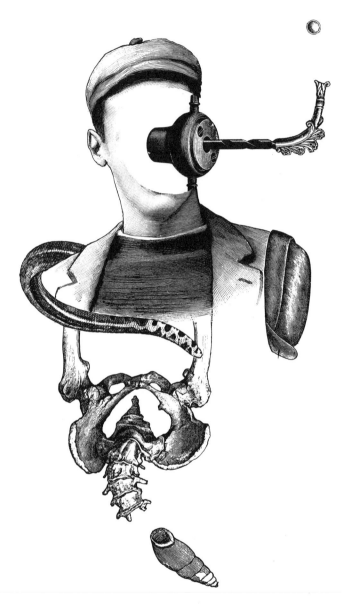

By burning the last plants and smoking madly . . .

By burning the last plants and smoking madly
I keep my white sphere aloft above
my pipe on a pillar of heated breath.
And with the same effort I expel
from the thoracic garden through a nether tube
the shell of dung, cleansing my streams of deceit
and exploding the blank world's fertility.

Quemando las últimas plantas y fumando locamente
mantengo mi blanca esfera en alto, por encima
de mi pipa sobre una columna de aliento sobrecalentado.
Y con el mismo esfuerzo expulso
del jardín torácico a través de un tubo infernal
el proyectil de estiércol, limpiando mis canales de todo fraude
y haciendo explotar la fertilidad del mundo vacío.

This is the way to make a perfect beast . . .

This is the way to make a perfect beast.
There are six pieces. The antelope is first.
Remove the foolish head with its razors of horn.

Este es el modo de formar la bestia perfecta.
Se toman seis pedazos. Primero está el antílope.
Se quita la cabeza ridícula con sus navajas de cuerno.

Add an old molar from the earth . . .

Add an old molar from the earth,
a tooth that never was in any mouth but God's.
Then a sea clamp to suppress the tides of blood.
In the midst, where the crushed herbs divide
into muscular heat and dung, install the philosopher
in his medicine cabinet. Open the crystal shutters
that are mirrors that are blinkers: make him stare
across white plains down the corridor of his reflection.
Now nothing is lacking but the lamp.
With this held high,

Se agrega una vieja muela de la tierra,
un diente que nunca estuvo en boca alguna, sino en la de Dios.
Luego el torniquete marino para detener las mareas de sangre.
En medio, donde las hierbas machacadas se dividen
en calor muscular y estiércol, se instala al filósofo
en su botiquín. Se abren las persianas de cristal
que son espejos, que son anteojeras: se le hace mirar fijo
a través de blancas llanuras, el corredor abajo de su reflejo.
Ahora sólo falta la lámpara.
Con ésta en alto,

. . . the new form of being . . .

                    the new form of being
can go through the night of no grass
seeking wisdom among rusting skeletons.

This is my people whom I have chosen for myself.
My people, who during a long drugged agony,
die of a pain they never feel. An exponential pain
that adds more zeroes to its force
through the series of uninterrupted nights.

                    la nueva forma, el nuevo ser
puede atravesar la noche sin pasto
buscando la sabiduría entre esqueletos oxidados.

Este es mi pueblo, mi pueblo elegido.
Mi pueblo, que durante una larga, drogada agonía,
muere de un dolor que nunca siente.
Dolor elevado a la enésima potencia
que agrega más ceros a su fuerza
al pasar series de noches ininterrumpidas.

Ceaselessly awake, I protect, comfort, and console.

Ceaselessly awake, I protect, comfort and console.
O river of morphine where the specimens float,
flowing down through the seven heads or hills
with lilies that trail their roots through the bronze reeds,
lilies digesting minerals and unfolding
fleshy ruffles of Parian marble white:
river, nourish my city, mistress of the world,
that leaps forward into centuries, bearing more death
each time she receives and heals again
her mortal wound.

Despierto sin cesar, yo protejo, doy ánimo y doy consuelo.
Oh río de morfina en donde flotan los especímenes
corriente abajo por las siete cabezas o colinas,
lirios que arrastran sus raíces a través de lengüetas de bronce,
lirios que digieren minerales, despliegan
carnosos vuelos fruncidos de blanco mármol pario:
río, nutre mi ciudad, dueña del mundo,
que salta adentrándose en los siglos, portando más muerte
cada vez que recibe y vuelve a sanar
su herida mortal.

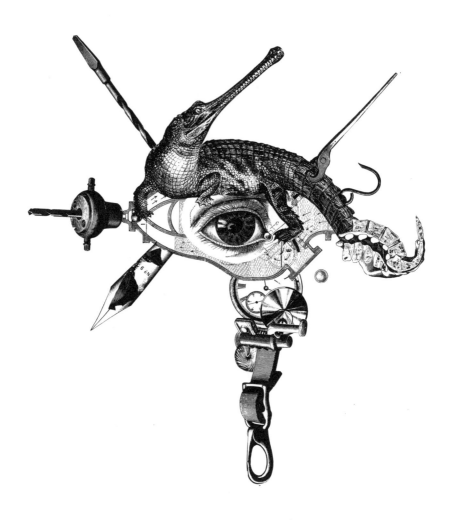

She observes measure in all things . . .

She observes measure in all things, creator
of the sex with three penises and one gonad.
For she sees clearly through the gauges of her face
that three and one is the ideal proportion
of pleasure (so little yet exists)
to person (of which there is too much).
As a root

Ella es mesurada en todas las cosas, creadora
del sexo con tres penes y una gónada.
Porque ve claramente por los manómetros de su rostro
que tres más uno es la proporción ideal
de placer (queda ya tan poco)
por persona (de las que hay demasía).
Como raíz

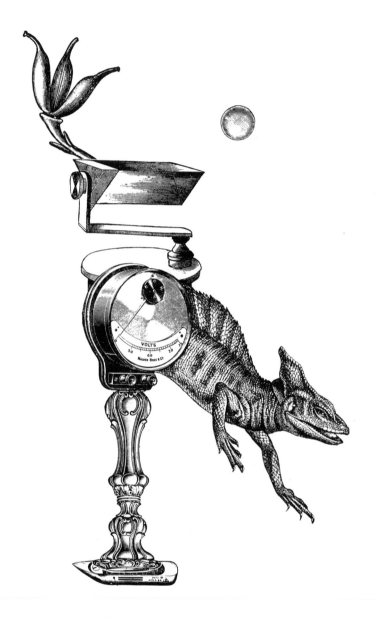

. . . her silver spoon bites deep . . .

her silver spoon bites deep
into the single grain that makes up all
this beach of machine parts, where she juggles
her fruits unabashed in the perfectly white light.

Then why, O circuit, O entropy, O pleasure,
does she bear this wet thing struggling in her side,
a child half born then clenched and pierced
through its navel by the jaws of a regretful womb?

su cuchara de plata penetra hondo
en la única veta que forma
toda esta playa de repuestos de máquinas,
donde ella sin vergüenza hace juegos de manos
con sus frutos en la luz perfectamente blanca.

Entonces ¿por qué, oh circuito, oh entropía, oh placer,
porta ella esta cosa húmeda que se agita en su costado,
un niño a medias nacido, luego atrapado y atravesado
en el ombligo por las mandíbulas de un vientre arrepentido?

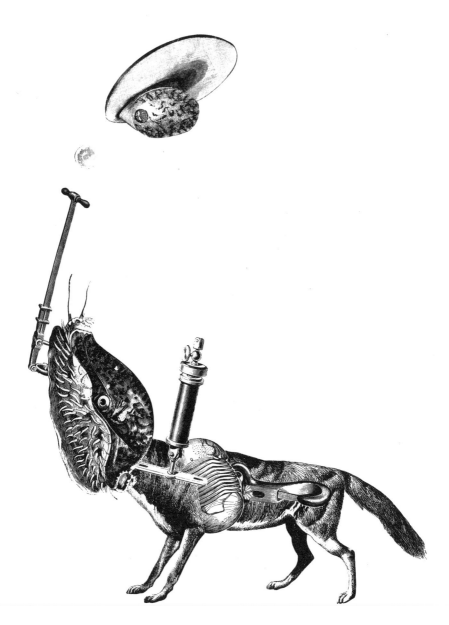

I sucked that mollusc woman with her salt . . .

I sucked that mollusc woman with her salt,
once, long ago, from the shell that is this world,
and made from it a cup of memory.

But my brothers, the cup has been empty
so many centuries,

Chupé ese molusco-mujer con su sal
antaño, hace tiempo, desde la concha que es este mundo
e hice con ello una copa de recuerdo.

Pero hermanos, la copa ha estado vacía
tantos siglos

. . . now I must grind your bodies . . .

now I must grind your bodies
to a bright juice. I know you are in pain,

but how remote, how calm you seem,
crushed and poured out beneath my seal
daily forever and ever on this white table.

O you,

que ahora debo moler los cuerpos
hasta convertirlos en zumo brillante. Sé que están dolidos

pero cuán remotos cuán sosegados parecen
aplastados y derramados bajo mi sello
diariamente por siempre jamás en esta blanca mesa.

Oh vosotros,

. . . lives destined to enter once again . . .

lives destined to enter once again
the emptied shell and perfect its emptiness:
remember me when you have reached the other shore.

que sois vidas destinadas a retornar de nuevo
a la concha abandonada, perfeccionar su oquedad:
acordáos de mí cuando lleguéis a la otra orilla.

And you, all webbed and struggling things . . .

And you, all webbed and struggling things,
I love you so much
that by my web and by my victory
I gather you in a white room closed to death.
You have no faith, you only ask
who will repay you for your loss:
the ecstasy, the sexual need
to prey, be captured, eat and die.
Then, contradicting yourselves, you say I honor
spiders, nothing but spiders.

Y vosotras, cosas tan enmarañadas os agitáis,
os amo tanto
que por mi telaraña y por mi victoria
os recojo en una sala blanca, cerrada a la muerte.
No tenéis fe, sólo preguntáis
quién recompensará vuestra pérdida:
el éxtasis, la necesidad sexual
de predar, ser capturados, comer y morir.
Luego, en contradicción a vosotros mismos, decís que yo rindo culto
a arañas, nada más que arañas.

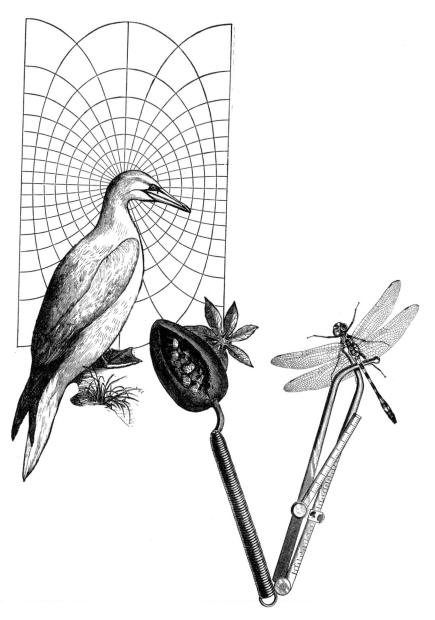

But look: for you, from the white desert . . .

But look: for you, from the white desert,
I have brought forth the world's last seven grass blades
like seven bound and tortured queens.
Here, too, is an amputated leaf.

And now my machine goes down the road alone,
betrayed, while I . . . Perhaps I was to heal,
to build. But indolence and pride have left me
only speech. And to speak in the rain of atoms:

Pero mirad: para vosotros, desde el desierto blanco
he hecho brotar las últimas siete hojas de hierba del mundo
como siete reinas amarradas y torturadas.
Hay también aquí una hoja amputada.

Y ahora mi máquina baja por el camino sola,
traicionada, mientras que yo . . . Quizás debía yo sanar,
construir. Pero la indolencia y el orgullo sólo me dejaron
el habla. Y hablar en la lluvia de átomos:

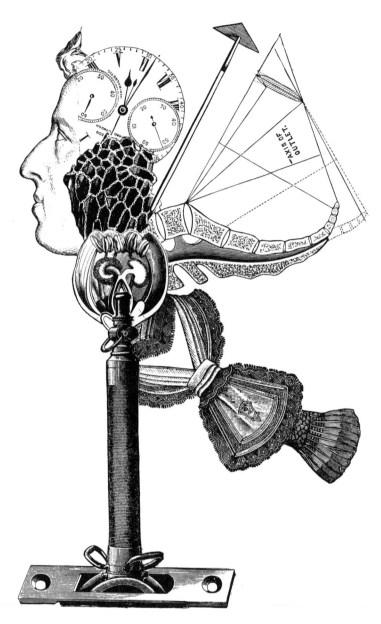

What is it but another mote in the eye?

what is it but another mote in the eye?
Just as the rain of letters falls
to form these lines, my sentence,
and then they return into the cloud
to come again, elsewhere, in other forms—
so I sleep, the hexameters are waves of honey
crested with clear plumes, are an atmosphere,
a labyrinth, foliage, architecture of light.
And now far into the night I work
to bring new terms that do not exist
to my thoughts, which I cannot grasp.
I sometimes think that if I could only rest

¿qué es, sino otra paja en el ojo?
Así como la lluvia de letras cae
hasta formar estos versos, mi sentencia,
y entonces retorna a la nube
para volver otra vez, en otro lugar, en otras formas—
así duermo, los hexámetros son olas de miel
coronadas de plumas claras, son una atmósfera,
un laberinto, follaje, arquitectura de luz.
Y ahora bien avanzada la noche trabajo
para imponer una nueva terminología que no existe,
a mis pensamientos que no alcanzo a aprehender.
A veces pienso que si yo tan sólo pudiera descansar

I would grow young again . . .

I would grow young again. . . .

With that he paused and looked up from his glass,
which is always full no matter how long he drinks.
He listened a while to the wind
and thus resumed.

                    Friends, I must leave you now.
It is already 5 a.m., the hour when flames
awaken in abandoned buildings.
I know my sister-wife is seeking me

llegaría a ser joven nuevamente . . .

Tras eso hizo una pausa y levantó los ojos de la copa,
siempre llena sin importar cuanto tomara.
Escuchó un rato al viento
y continuó así.

                    Amigos, ahora debo dejarlos.
Ya amanece, hora en que las llamas
despiertan en los edificios abandonados.
Sé que mi mujer-hermana me anda buscando

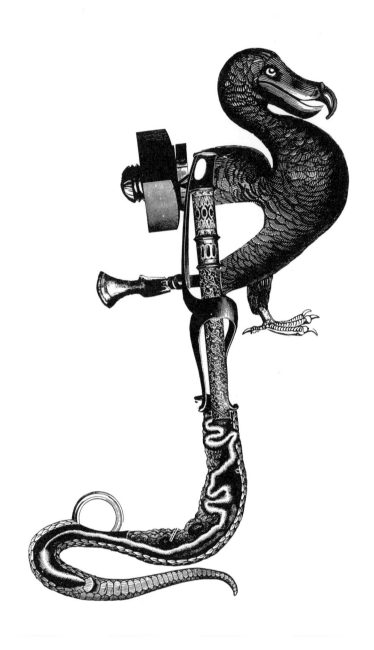

. . .for someone begins to torture birds: I hear them scream . . .

for someone begins to torture birds: I hear them scream.
Each dawn as she comes for me
she crosses the park where the species, obsolete,
are shut in their cages of wood,
and she lifts the heavy stone of being from one or another.

porque alguien está empezando a torturar las aves: las oigo gritar.
Cada alba, cuando ella viene por mí,
cruza el parque en que las especies obsoletas
se hallan encerradas en su jaula de madera,
y levanta la pesada losa del ser de una u otra.

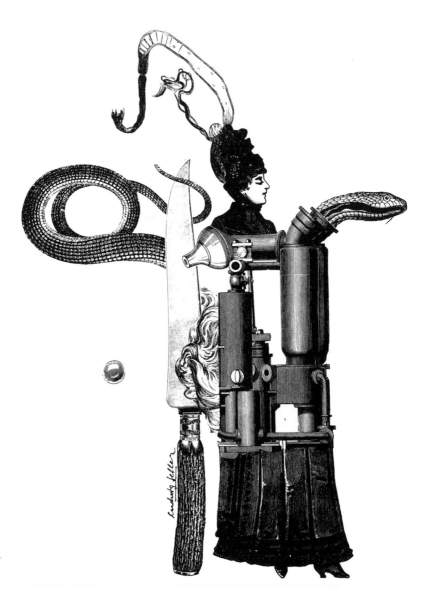

I can hear her footsteps now, the stiff leg she drags . . .

I can hear her footsteps now, the stiff leg she drags
behind her through the flooded lanes:
her wooden leg which is returning to life,
which puts down shallow roots at each step.
Without rest she must pull it from the ground
to avoid becoming a tentacle of the earth.
Night and day I hear her in the dark
and she issues in my song as mist from a crevice.

Ahora oigo sus pasos, la tiesa pierna que arrastra
detrás de sí por los senderos inundados:
su pierna de madera que retorna a la vida,
que echa raíces superficialies a cada paso.
Sin descanso debe arrancarla del suelo
para no convertirse en un tentáculo de la tierra.
Noche y día la oigo en la oscuridad
y ella surge de mi canto como la neblina de una hendidura.

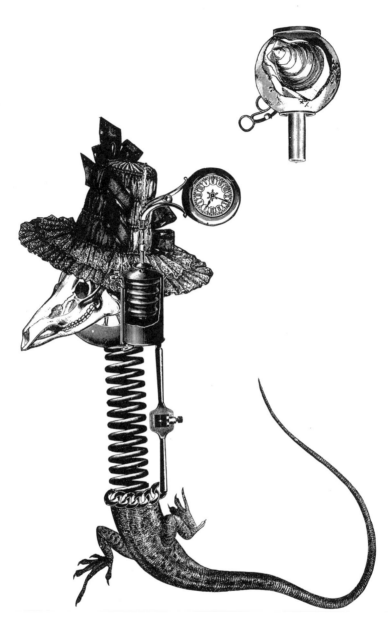

I hear her coming to find if I will go down . . .

I hear her coming to find if I will go down.
But friends, at last I know, and I am translated
to a bubble that a drowned breath
pushes up to be flooded with infinite gold.

On that note he left us and we saw no more
of Sisyphus until the following night.

La oigo venir para enterarse si he de bajar.
Pero, amigos, finalmente lo sé, soy trasladado
a una burbuja que un aliento ahogado
empuja arriba para ser inundado con oro infinito.

Con esas palabras nos dejó y no supimos más
de Sísifo hasta la noche siguiente.

Afterword
by Susana Wald

For years Ludwig Zeller has worked in collaboration with other artists, visual artists for the most part. Often his poems would comment on the imagery of painters and sculptors. He has also combined his visual work—his collages—with the paintings and drawings of others, and he has illustrated books of poetry.

The rather unusual collaboration between A.F. Moritz and Ludwig Zeller awakened my curiosity. Here was the case of two poets, close in feeling, who came together and decided to share different expressions of a similar impulse, one visually and the other verbally. So I resolved to ask how each saw his own work in relation to the other's. The following is a part of the resulting interview.

S.W.: Mr. Moritz, what do you find to be the point of coincidence between the poem and the collages?

A.F. Moritz: I think they share the myth of the bachelor machines as their basis. The poem and collages both contend with the new world. Machines have appeared from within each being like tumors. The new hybrid creatures are dominated by the machine: the animal is the suffering residue. And the machines are bachelors: they interact, but they don't communicate at all. So here is a new botany for this world, a new zoology, topography, history, and a new law. I'd also say a new sexuality, except that now the law includes sexuality.

Animals are the chief victims here. I think it's worth mentioning that our first idea was to do a bestiary. But it became an explorer's narrative, a journey to a new continent that turns out to be the very ship we're on, the Ark we've enclosed ourselves in, as we try to save what we've made of ourselves by translating it, transporting it.

There's a satiric as well as a tragic side to this. The machines are actually dominated, in a way, by the animals. They're only imitations of the animals. For all their superior power, they don't succeed in being in the least original; they're only extensions—crude metaphors—of limbs, brains, nerves, sense organs, the body's tubes and ducts. They are parodies.

S.W.: Mr. Zeller, do you perceive in Moritz's voice an echo of the imagery in your collages?

L.Z.: Over all, these images were created with a technique quite similar to that of automatic writing and they originate from a tradition having many precedents in the contemporary world. One also finds this tradition in the ancient world where one culture is overlaid on or joined to another, as in the case of whole cities like Alexandria or Cairo, the latter built out of stones taken from the pyramids; or in the case of Venice, built from elements collected from many cultures. Looking at references in the poem to my images, I see with enthusiasm the poet finding his way in this veritable morass and coming out of it expressing his own self. It is quite curious, for example, that in the poetic language the somewhat obscene insistence on the animal imagery of the collages disappears to be replaced by a verbal cosmic vision of the poet. This verbal "image" seems very important to me because it is supported by a story in which Moritz has chosen to use a form of literary collage: various ideas are introduced, opinions offered, the meaning of life questioned. This kind of query, this manner of questioning the ultimate meaning of creation, is especially interesting. In this sense there is an aching, but personal echo in Moritz's voice.

S.W.: I have a feeling as I go through the poem that the idea of harmony is being abolished.

A.F.M.: Yes, there's a practical abolition of harmony in the poem, but not an ideal abolition of it. The poem tries to preserve the hope that harmony can return in a new form. Both poem and collage carry in them—in the Ark—many reminiscences of the formal harmonies of the past. That's obvious in Ludwig's work, but the poem contains many collage elements too: echoes of fable and history, philosophical and theological ideas, paraphrases from sources such as the sayings of the desert fathers, documents of imperial Egypt, Dante, Virgil, Lucretius. For me the idea of shipwreck comes from Leopardi and Ortega, the idea of the sister-wife comes from Shelley. Many elements of classic English literature are present in the versification, the story, and so on. For instance, the poem is a dramatic monologue spoken by Sisyphus that is held in a very brief frame—only the first four and the last two lines—but it implies a whole story that encloses Sisyphus's story. The great original here is "The Rime of the Ancient Mariner," and there are many allusions of form, as well as similarities and contradictions. The story of *Phantoms* is not told on dry land, at a reflective distance; it's told on the haunted ship in the heart of the disaster. The idle passersby in this case seize the ancient mariner and force his story out of him—and they remain completely unconscious, unmoved, unimpressed, before, during and after—not at all like the Wedding Guest, who woke "a wiser man."

Things like that point to an end to harmony. But at the same time they're a memory of harmony that amounts to a commitment.

S.W.: Mr. Zeller, is it the presence or the absence of harmony that you find more obvious between text and images?

L.Z.: Let's talk first about the presence. I believe that there is an evident correlation between text and images. There is a re-creation of the world, an ontological conquest of the possibilities of creating an ultimate form that I continually struggle with when I make my collages. I see in Moritz a very similar preoccupation when he queries this ultimate form, because the essence of perfection cannot be touched by human beings.

Secondly, the matter of the absence of harmony. I would say that in all of my "artistic activity" (and therefore in these images) I constantly return to an archetype that worries me: a female image of the divine. Maybe it is a way of making something sacred out of all that is female, be it animal or machine in constant metamorphosis towards a new model, or, be it in poetry, towards the word that illuminates all. In this respect I find Moritz more austere than myself—it is obvious that in this poem about the fate of mankind he has opted for extreme severity—reducing the language of love to a middle tone of the narrative without the contrasts and stridencies that are natural to my being.

S.W.: In your view, Mr. Moritz, what is the most characteristic, the most evident feature of the collages?

A.F.M.: First of all, there's the impression they give of restriction and deformity. Many of them create new beings that seem to be the result of a vivisectionist's experiment. But this Dr. Moreau isn't a biologist, he's an engineer. Then there's the very moving expressions of the victims, especially the innocent animal blankness and sadness of the lizards and antelopes, who awaken and find themselves changed and removed from their homes, imprisoned in a new form of existence. These creatures exist on a blank white background, and it seems impossible to imagine a world where their useless shapes and organs and limbs might function. There are collages that are spread all over the page, scattered, and some with far-flung pieces connected together by thin, fragile devices. This provokes a particular kind of horror and pity, like that we feel for a worm, or perhaps a wasp, whose body seems nearly cut in two. It's horrible because it's unknowingly trapped in its fragility, and that's how it menaces us: by showing us something about ourselves.

Another thing that strikes me about the collages is their baroque quality. You can easily list all the elements in them: animals, men and women, springs, watches, gauges, screws, threaded tubes, various small tools and so on. And yet these few things combine into a seemingly infinite number of threatening, mystifying shapes. There's a continuous change which somehow never manages to make any difference because it can't break out of the limits strictly determined and defined by the elements that compose it. Here is the characteristic that is shared by mechanism and by certain human dreams.

S.W.: Mr. Zeller, do you find sexual references in Moritz's poem, and are these parallel to your images?

L.Z.: Novalis said a very precise thing, that all works of art could be reinterpreted. All poems, all visual images, should be rich enough in possibilities to be able to withstand various analyses. In the collages, especially in this series, few references are made to the feminine. There are two or three female figures; the rest of the collages are composed of images of animals and machines. Although the poem has a more evident cultural background, its juxtaposition of references, myths and like ideas reveals a parallel to the images. One doesn't pretend that these are seen as if in a mirror, because they correspond to the verbal world while the collages are visual images. But the parallel exists, this is evident. A different language is used. It would have been absurd to repeat the same figures in speech. Moritz's work has been to search for occult connections that exist, to read the secret message of these images and to express them in his own way.

S.W.: If you perceive a dilemma that is presented by Ludwig's images, what would you say is the solution to this dilemma?

A.F.M.: On an objective level, the images show how man presumes to rework the world. On the oneiric level, they represent how man has come to seem to himself in the process. The collages say not only that we cut up the world and mix it with machine parts; we find a metaphor for ourselves and an objectification of our dreams in the machine. We make machines more powerful than ourselves, and then we feel like inept machines. But in Ludwig's images we see that machines are extensions of the problems of the body, not its glory. They finalize that vertiginous morning sensation when you wake up and suddenly say to yourself, how did I get here, why am I in this shape? I'm something infinitely freer and more magnificent than this. I've awakened into a nightmare and now I have to reawaken, or truly awaken. I have to wake up. The shock that makes us want to wake up, to reawaken to our true selves: that's the gift of Ludwig's collages. And that's the germ of a solution to the dilemma they pose.

I would also say that, despite everything, they celebrate the natural world. These animals, infiltrated and overcome by the machine, look out with a sadness that rebukes us. And there's also a rebuke in the unconscious complacency of the men and women who've suffered the same fate. We're reminded of other powers, other potentials, other possible directions, that we haven't even recognized, let alone explored—human potentials that aren't satisfied by the world we're making, or by the worlds we imagine.

S.W.: Mr. Zeller, do you perceive a dilemma in Moritz's poem? Do you see a solution to it?

L.Z.: This is a complex question because a poem, a collection of images, an activity that is driven in a certain direction also communicates a philosophy of life, the feeling of being in the world. To put it concisely, I don't see in Moritz a region, a country or a language, I see in him an immense migration to a zone of bones, of essences. In his dense and generous humanity he advances into the innermost core of his being. And his display of verbal elements does not seem ostentatious because he uses similar ideas, resonances of sacred books or of the classics such as Lucretius or Virgil. When talking about dilemmas, I feel they are latent in all creative people and if I pose the question of a solution I think each of us carries it in himself; in my case I find this solution in the world of love, there is no other exit, even if other names are found for it.

S.W.: Were you expecting a question that didn't come?

A.F.M.: Well, one thing that might seem curious, I thought, is the way both poem and collages combine the visionary and a certain sarcasm. I think that so-called "vision" is always largely critical—look at the Biblical prophets—because the sense of what we *could* be so strongly implies what we're *not*. On one level, *Phantoms* is a satire, one that looks at the history and thought of the human race as wrong turns and shibboleths. And *Phantoms* implicates not only the machine civilization, but the culture that people often claim is separate from and opposed to it. Technological regimentation springs from the same source as its supposed antidotes, the various forms of vitalism and aestheticism.

S.W.: Is there a question that you would like to ask Ludwig in reference to the images?

A.F.M.: Since I took the collage series he gave me and rearranged it until I finally arrived at the order of the poem, I wonder how he responds to this experience of being treated the same way he treats his old magazines.

S.W.: Have you been bothered by the fact that Moritz has rearranged your world in his way?

L.Z.: No. First of all, Moritz is my friend; secondly he is a poet who has worked very closely with me. I gave him a set of images. That he has rearranged them according to his taste is the natural fate of these images. Anyhow, in any kind of order they will find a new magnetism, a new tension....

Ludwig Zeller is prominent in both Latin American poetry and international surrealism. His recent books of poems include *Salvar la poesía quemar las naves* (Mexico City, 1988; 2nd ed. 1994) and *Tatuajes del fantasma* (Mexico City, 1993). Zeller has exhibited his collages in scores of one-man and group shows throughout North and South America and western Europe. Before coming to Canada in 1971, he was curator of the Chilean Ministry of Education Art Gallery (1952-70). Recently he has been an exhibitor at the Venice Biennial (1986), a featured poet of the Rotterdam International Poetry Festival (1987), and the featured poet and artist of the Guadalajara International Book Fair (1991).

A. F. Moritz is the author of eight books of poems; his poetry has received the Award in Literature of the American Academy and Institute of Arts and Letters, and Canada Council, Guggenheim Foundation and Ingram Merrill Foundation fellowships. He has translated books by Ludwig Zeller including *In the Country of the Antipodes: Selected Poems 1964-1979* (Oakville, Ont., 1979) and *The Ghost's Tattoos* (Oakville, Ont., 1989).

Phantoms in the Ark/Fantasmas en el arca originated when Zeller asked Moritz to write a long poem in dialogue with a series of collages in progress. The poem was begun using a group of passages already on hand from Moritz's project *Lucretius in the New World,* influenced by Zeller's poetry. As the passages grew in response to the collages, they were arranged in dialogue with them. On completion, Zeller gave the collage-poem its title. *Phantoms in the Ark* concludes *Lucretius in the New World,* other parts of which appear in *Black Orchid* (1981), *The Tradition* (1986) and *Song of Fear* (1992).